WHEN WE CAN'T FIND GOD, GOD FINDS US

JULIE DECTIS

WESTBOW
P R E S S®
A DIVISION OF THOMAS NELSON
& ZONDERVAN

WestBow Press books may be ordered through booksellers or by contacting:

WestBow Press
A Division of Thomas Nelson & Zondervan
1663 Liberty Drive
Bloomington, IN 47403
www.westbowpress.com
1 (866) 928-1240

THE HOLY BIBLE, NEW INTERNATIONAL VERSION®,
NIV® Copyright © 1973, 1978, 1984, 2011 by Biblica, Inc.®
Used by permission. All rights reserved worldwide.

ISBN: 978-1-5127-6134-4 (sc)
ISBN: 978-1-5127-6133-7 (e)

Library of Congress Control Number: 2016917404

Print information available on the last page.

WestBow Press rev. date: 10/19/2016

To God:

Thank You for never giving up on me. Thank You for your never-ending grace and mercy.

To Peter:

Thank you for your continual love and support. You have an amazing work ethic and love for God and family. I am so thankful every day that God chose you for me.

Verse you exemplify: "But when you pray, go into your room, close the door and pray to your Father, who is unseen. Then your Father, who sees what is done in secret, will reward you" (Matthew 6:6).

To Alexa:

Thank you for constantly challenging me to look deeper. Without the amazing story you brought to our family, this book would not be possible. Your wit and outgoing, positive personality have been motivation to many!

Verse you exemplify: "Blessed is the one who perseveres under trial because, having stood the test, that person will receive the crown of life that the Lord has promised to those who love him" (James 1:12).

To Nicole:

Thank you for being the amazing blessing you are. God certainly knew we would need your love and energy to complete our family. From the four-year-old girl who wouldn't leave the alley until she could ride her bike without training wheels to the amazing woman you are today doing God's work, your drive and perseverance never cease to amaze me!

Verse you exemplify: "I can do all this through him who gives me strength" (Philippians 4:13).

To Mom:

Thank you for loving me unconditionally; for always being my biggest supporter; and for teaching me that I could do anything through hard work and perseverance. Most of all thank you for having the courage to recognize and break the cycle of dysfunction and addiction for me as well as future generations.

Prayer you live by: God, grant me the serenity to accept the things I cannot change, courage to change the things I can, and wisdom to know the difference.

To Grandmom Daddona:

Thank you for teaching me to love everyone and to serve joyfully.

Verse you exemplified: "For we are God's handiwork, created in Christ Jesus to do good works, which God prepared in advance for us to do" (Ephesians 2:10).

I am grateful for the priests and pastors who have helped shape my life and my writing through God. Also, to my dear friends and family for your constant support and encouragement. Last but not least, to all who read and reread for proofing and editing purposes.

A special thanks to my amazing cover design team. You exceeded all my expectations and captured in art what I'm trying to convey in words: Chris Starwalt for the overall design; Jen Starwalt for the artwork; Steve Kandianis for the graphic; and Peter Newton for the photo.

Contents

Chapter 1

I Was Lost, but He Found Me

Looking back on various events in my life, several stand out in my mind where God was trying to lead me to Him. My mind was not yet open, and my free will was running wild and rampant. When I was sixteen God put a wonderful friend in my path. Her name is Mindy. Mindy's mom knew I was a free spirit who didn't know the Lord. Mrs. K would always welcome me into her home with open arms, and as Mindy and I would walk out the door on a Saturday night, she would say to me, "Julie Daddona, I'm praying for you!" She is the first person in my life that I think was truly praying for me with all her heart.

God put Mrs. K in my life to begin planting seeds. When I didn't start growing, He knew He had to do something drastic. He uses our worst hardships to bring us closer to Him. He was determined to find me!

Fast-forward ten years. When my husband, Peter, and I decided to have a baby, my biggest fear was having a child with a disability. Well, talk about what you think, so shall it be.

I was seven months pregnant with Alexa when I left my job as an engineer. From that moment of my pregnancy I enjoyed the peace and calm I felt within me. In fact, I'd never felt so much peace until that point.

March 5, 1993. Peter and I were so excited when Alexa was born. The first thing that came to my mind when I saw her was, *Thank You, God, for this healthy baby.* She was so alert. In fact, to this day I have never seen a baby more aware and interested in her surroundings than Alexa was. She slept very little, but she hardly ever cried. She would just look around as if she were taking everything in. She always looked like she had a knowing about her. It was as if Alexa knew much more than any of us did about all aspects of life. My mom said from the day she was born, "This is a very wise old soul in a new body." I think this was God giving her in cognition what she lacked physically.

I thanked God every day for her. I believed I had attracted this calm and serene child because I was so calm and serene during the last months of my pregnancy. Little did I know …

Our life revolved around Alexa. I didn't go back to work. Instead I decided to finish the MBA degree I had started nights when I was working. Alexa appeared to be developing very typically until about seven or eight months. By ten months I started to ask the pediatrician questions because Alexa wasn't crawling, didn't pull up on anything, and didn't put herself into a sitting position. Her feet also turned in quite a bit. Every month I went back to the doctors telling them I didn't think Alexa was progressing. They kept telling me she was just lazy, that she needed motivation. At the same time this was going on, I became pregnant again. It was a surprise to us. We were starting to think it was time for me to go back to work since money was getting tight. I was actually a little scared of having another child. Eventually I realized it was certainly God's blessing!

Finally, when she was sixteen months old, I took Alexa to a developmental pediatrician. She was diagnosed with spinal muscular atrophy (SMA) within a week.

Peter and I were devastated. We thought we were both going crazy and that it was a bad dream from which we would awaken. I remember sitting in the office with the doctor. Alexa was standing along a bookshelf of toys. I was looking at her with tears streaming down my face, barely hearing what the doctor was saying—will never walk, will be in a wheelchair. My emotions were going wild. All our hopes and dreams up until that point had been shattered. I started blaming myself. Was it because I was so stressed when I was working? Was it because I chewed a piece of gum with NutraSweet in it? I was looking for reasons everywhere.

Then the doctor said something about it being genetic. I was twenty-six weeks pregnant. I turned to her and asked the question I feared most: "What about this baby?"

"I'm sorry," she said, "the baby has a twenty-five percent chance of having the disease also." More tears. Panic. Anxiety. I felt as if a three hundred–pound person was sitting on my chest. I was gasping for air. *Okay. This must be a bad dream. Time to wake up now!* I couldn't take the tremendous pain.

I was asked if I wanted genetic testing. My choice was absolutely not. It didn't matter at this point. If the baby had it, she had it. There was no changing that. The next fourteen weeks were filled with tremendous fear and pain. We went to doctor after doctor and therapy after therapy. We had an average of three to four appointments a week for Alexa. I cried every day. I cried for Alexa, for my unborn child, and for me and the life I was now to live. I was angry and hated everything, most of all God. How could He have done this to me? Was I that bad of a person to deserve this? It was as if I was going through the Kubler-Ross death and dying stages I studied in high school—denial, anger, bargaining, depression, and finally acceptance, which I thought I would never see.

October 28, 1994. Nicole was born. The doctor who diagnosed Alexa was at the hospital within three hours of the delivery. She checked Nicole from head to toe. She told me, "Nicole appears to be fine, but we won't be certain until she starts developing motor skills. You can still do genetic testing, you know." This meant taking blood from Alexa, and after having the lab technicians stick her five times for preadmission testing before her diagnostic surgery, I couldn't do it. (They never did get blood from her.)

"I waited this long and I will continue to wait. I can't do that to Alexa."

Little Nicole came out as anyone could imagine—like a ball of stress. She cried day and night for the first five months, and I had no one to blame but myself. I had passed my stress to my baby. I was exhausted. Alexa was very sick that winter and needed a ton of care. Nicole was left to cry because I couldn't hold her while I was doing Alexa's breathing treatments and chest physical therapy. There were many days when I really thought I was going crazy, and I was afraid I would hurt the children because I couldn't deal with the stress and exhaustion. Some days I would call Peter at work crying because I couldn't take Nicole's crying. She just wouldn't stop. I would have him come home for fear I was reaching the end of my limits.

Over the next two years, I did the best I could balancing the demands of Alexa with the challenges of Nicole. Alexa always had the best of care and grew into a very cheerful, loving child who captured everyone's heart upon first meeting. She was extremely intelligent, singing the ABC song by eighteen months with perfect diction and recognizing every letter of the alphabet by name by the time she was two and a half.

Soon after Alexa's second birthday, we were sitting in the family room—Alexa, Peter, and I. Alexa looked at the ceiling and said, "Mommy, look, I see Jesus up there."

I looked up, astonished at what she was saying. I said, "You do? Is there anyone with Jesus?"

She said, "Yes, I see Mary too; Mary is with Him."

I asked her what Mary looked like, and she changed the subject and went on with our previous discussion. We never really discussed God, Jesus, or Mary too much with her. When we did, we mostly used the Greek names, especially for Mary, which would be *Panagia* in Greek. I had always known Alexa had a special knowing about her, and this incident confirmed my thoughts.

Nicole got more and more active, and she only walked for about two weeks. Then she ran. She developed more and more anger toward Alexa and the attention she got not only from me but from everyone else too. I felt bad for her, but I didn't know how to make it better. I was constantly feeling torn between the two children—Nicole's emotional needs or Alexa's constant physical needs. But I had a knowing deep inside that the children had some part in choosing the life they did because there were things that only Peter and I could teach them. There were goals they needed to achieve that only we could help them achieve.

Peter and I felt the constant stress of all this on our marriage. I wasn't going to have my family fall apart anymore. By the spring of 1995, I'd had enough. I went back to the principles my mom had taught me through my adolescent years. I began going to church with her, and I started to try meditating and reading some of the books she had given me through the years. I pulled out a book she had given me while I was in college. The title was *Your Erroneous Zones* by Dr. Wayne Dyer. I read a couple of chapters, then put it down. I remember going to see the author speak at some conference in Philadelphia with a bunch of other spiritual-type speakers several years before. But I just didn't get it. He was way over my head. My brother was really into him, but I couldn't see what the fascination was.

It was around my second winter with both children, the winter of 1995–96, that people would often ask me "How do you do it?"

I didn't know how I kept going and going. I knew that God, Alexa, and Nicole chose Peter and me for some reason, although some days I wondered what that reason could be. I never quite knew how to answer this question. It was really hard some days, especially when Alexa was sick and I was up for days at a time without sleeping. Or I was running her to therapies and doctors' appointments an average of three to four times a week, trying to make sense of what the doctors were saying with Nicole creating havoc in the examining room with us. Or when my back hurt so bad from lifting Alexa that I didn't know if I could get her from her wheelchair to the potty or car seat one more time.

Even though it was hard, I really didn't mind caring for Alexa. In fact, I got more gratification out of my children than anything in my life. "I just do it," I would tell people, not really believing inside that was the right answer. I knew there was more of a reason than what Nike came up with as a marketing gimmick. But I just couldn't figure it out. Why did I do it?

I continued to try meditation and most of the time, if nothing else, got just a little peace out of it. In spring of 1996 Wayne Dyer came to Allentown to speak. My mom asked me if I wanted to go. I wasn't thrilled with the idea but said, "Sure, why not?" I was growing and by this point, understanding that there are no coincidences. I was sitting in the auditorium at Cedar Crest College wondering what this guy had in store for me. Little did I know that was the day that was to change my attitude and outlook on everything around me.

As he spoke, I kept saying to myself, "I'm here for a reason. I'm right where I'm supposed to be."

Wayne spoke of a woman, Kaye O'Bara, who had been taking care of her daughter who had been in a coma for more than twenty-six years. He spoke of her unconditional love for her daughter and what it was like for them. Wayne Dyer's next words were to change my life forever. He said when Kaye was asked why she does this, her answer was, "Because God asked me to, and God never asks you to do something you can't do." When I heard these words come from Wayne's mouth, I wanted to jump up and shout, "That's it! That's why I do it!" It may seem like an obvious answer, but to me it was a revelation. It was the answer to the question I and so many others had been asking. Because God asked me to. Again, He was determined to find me!

I had an immediate bond with this woman, Kaye O'Bara. I sent a letter with a check and asked to please be sent a book. I read the book while I was sitting in a hospital waiting for Alexa to come out of surgery. It was an incredible story that touched me. I found so many parallels between my life and the life of this woman, although I could never compare to the saintliness she had about her.

Fall 1996. Alexa was now three and a half. She started asking me really complex questions about God: where we go when we die, when is she going to die, when am I going to die, who will be there when we get there, where was she before she came to live with me. They didn't end. My simple answers weren't enough for her. She kept on and on. I always answered them the best I could. I knew my answers weren't satisfactory to her, but it was all I knew. I felt bad because I knew she was beyond me and I felt like I should have these answers for her, but I didn't know where to go to get them.

One day around this same time, Alexa was at school and was very sad. When the teacher asked her why she seemed so sad, she wouldn't tell her. She was playing with a doll and started hitting the doll, saying, "Die, baby, die. It's time for you to die." The physical therapist came in after this had happened, and the teacher told her privately what Alexa had done. The therapist then told Alexa she had some work to do in the other room and asked if Alexa wanted to come with her. She gave Alexa a baby to play with, and Alexa repeated the same behavior. She asked Alexa why the baby needed to die. Alexa said, "Because her legs don't work, and babies die if their legs don't work."

When I picked her up from school, she told me she had a sad day at school. When I asked her why, she wouldn't tell me. The next day the therapist told me what had happened.

I was really upset and knew I wasn't satisfying Alexa's questions with my answers over the past month or so. That night when I was putting Alexa to bed, I asked her, "Alexa, where do you think you will go when you die?'

Alexa said, "To heaven."

I asked, "Is it a nice place or a not-so-nice place?"

Alexa said, "A nice place."

I said, "Tell me what it's like there."

Alexa replied, "God is there."

I asked, "Do you want to go there?"

Alexa yelled, *"No!"*

I asked, "Why not?"

Alexa replied, "I don't want to leave you."

I asked, "When do you think you will go there?"

Alexa said, "Soon."

"Why?" I asked.

Alexa replied, "Because my legs don't work, and kids whose legs don't work die."

Then she burst into tears, sobbing and sobbing. I didn't know where all this was coming from. We focused so much on what to do to keep her healthy and didn't discuss that she could die or would die. I explained to her that many years ago kids with SMA did die young, because the doctors didn't have the technology that they have today. But today we have lots of good doctors, medicines, and equipment that if she got really, really sick we would use. She started calming down a little.

Then Alexa asked, "Will I ever die?"

I replied, "Yes, someday you will die, when you and God decide it's time."

Alexa asked, "Who will die first, me or you?"

I answered, "I don't know."

She started crying really hard again, saying she didn't want me to die.

That fall Wayne Dyer came to speak again, and I went to hear him. He introduced his CD *Meditations for Manifestation.* I bought the CD and started to do the meditations on occasion, not regularly. I also started listening to some of his work on tape.

I would listen to it in the car. Sometimes Alexa would be in the car with me. She started listening intently to what he was saying. It got to the point that she would request his tapes over her kids' tapes. She would say, "Mommy, put Wayne Dyer in. He's so peaceful." I began to realize that she was getting the answers to the questions she had from these tapes—all the questions I could not completely answer. I then started seeking out more and more information—anything I might be able to find that would help her on her journey.

In my search for Christ, when Alexa was six, I would get up before the kids and would read various Christian books. (I had not yet accepted Jesus as my Lord and Savior at this point.) Since Alexa was on a spiritual quest and wise beyond her years, she asked if she could wake early with me and read together. We were reading a book about Mary, mother of God (who we call *Panagia* in Greek). Alexa asked me where she was buried and if we could go there to pray for a cure. I explained to her that Mary was not buried because she ascended into heaven, as did Jesus, but there was a tomb for her in Israel. Alexa asked if we could go there to pray for a cure for SMA.

The next sequence of events culminate, literally, from one miracle to another. I told my husband what Alexa had asked, and we thought there was no way we could financially afford to do such a thing. I got the kids off to school, and I went to church. I spoke with Father Michael, asking his opinion on the matter. He said that it would be a wonderful blessing and I should pray about it. Now … my prayer life was pretty poor at that point in my life. Remember, I was going through the motions of a believer, but I was not a believer in my heart yet at this point.

I went into the church and started to pray. I asked God, "If this is the right thing to do, please make it clear to me." I walked out of church, got in my car, and my cell phone rang. It was Peter. He told me he had just walked out of his mom's office, and she had money from his Yaya that she was saving to give him at the right time and this was it. She wanted us to use it to go to Israel. God couldn't have made it clearer! He wasn't giving up. He was determined to find me!

Within a few weeks, we were off to Israel, along with Father Michael. While we were in Israel, Alexa became very ill with a respiratory infection. Respiratory infections are the leading cause of death in children with SMA. On this particular day, we had gone to the tomb of Mary. There was a church service going on, so we couldn't actually go into the tomb that day. That night was the worst night of Alexa's illness. I was exhausted from traveling and being up in the nights with Alexa. The hotel rooms were small, so Alexa and I were in a room by ourselves. Peter and Nicole had a separate room. I was sitting awake in bed watching Alexa take each breath when a vision appeared before me. It was Mary! She told me not to worry; everything was going to be okay. She said we should take Alexa back to the tomb, lay her on it, and pray. The next day we went back to the tomb and did as Mary instructed, then took Alexa to the hospital. Alexa did recover.

I'm very thick headed, you see, because even after this experience, I still was not a believer in my heart. I searched for another year. I kept my mind open and began a Bible study with my dear friend, Laura. It was the summer of 2001 through that Bible study that I found Christ. Through Laura's explanation of the gospel of John, I learned that all I had to do was pray for Christ to forgive me of my sins and reveal Himself to me and He would do it. I prayed that prayer in my car on my way down the highway that night. So on a warm summer night, at the age of thirty-four, I was finally home! When I couldn't find God, God found me!

This was when the living and learning really began. I was

a new Christian, and I had (and will always have) so much to learn so I could teach it to my children. I needed to teach them the love of Jesus and how to be an example of that love. It was a very difficult thing to do when I myself didn't quite understand it. The following pages are what I discovered as I continued to help my children grow emotionally and spiritually.

Notes

Chapter 2

Gratitude—Giving Thanks

Every morning when I wake up, I am grateful. I am grateful for what I have and what I don't have, what I have seen and what I haven't seen. I am grateful because I have faith and I trust God. I trust that I am right where I'm supposed to be when I'm supposed to be there. When I hear people complaining about what they have or don't have, my heart feels sad because if we just look at the good in our lives, we will have peace.

I thank God for what I have every day.

I start with being grateful to God for being a part of my life and gracing me with His presence in my heart. Then I move to being grateful for my good health and well-being and the healthy food I have to nourish my body.

In the twenty-five years we have been married, my husband has come to my bedside and kissed me good-bye every single morning before he left for work. I am so grateful to my husband, for the love we have, for all the things he does around the house, like cleaning up the kitchen and mowing the lawn, the fact that he spends time with our children each and every day. He is such a good father. He's a hard worker; he works many hours in a day, earns a good living, and still has time for us at the end of the day.

I am grateful for my two beautiful children who want to please us and God. They are so intelligent, and they do well in school. As I become more and more grateful and appreciative of their strength and abilities, the more strengths and abilities they develop.

Don't get me wrong. They aren't perfect. They bicker and argue as they figure out communication skills and what works or doesn't work. I'm sure that one of the biggest problems in today's society is the expectation that siblings will not get along. I hear, "Oh, they fight all the time. That's what sisters and brothers do." If that is the expectation, then that is what will occur. The expectation in our house is that everyone gets along, and everyone loves each other. We try to demonstrate God's love to them so they see the example and love each other.

I am grateful for Alexa having SMA. I know it may sound funny to you for me to be grateful for such a horrible disease. But I don't look at it that way. God sent me these children to help me be closer to Him. Without SMA, I don't think I would have even a fraction of the relationship I have with God today.

> *Sometimes what we think might be a bad thing is really just God's wake-up call to have us take a look at our lives and how we are living them.*

Sometimes what we think might be a bad thing is really just God's wake-up call to have us take a look at our lives and how we are living them. I was living my life as a selfish, grumpy, unthankful, ungrateful, negative person. I could find all the negative in everything positive. As a result, I felt stressed all the time. God was trying to get through to me in other ways, but I wasn't listening. Only when I turned around and started to find the good in everything did more good follow.

When I became grateful, wonderful things started to consume my life. I felt more secure and assured about decision making. I was calmer and more at peace. My children were behaving better and better. Their academic excellence increased, along with their self-esteem. Then came the monetary and material things. My husband's earning potential doubled. We were able to afford a wheelchair van. We built our dream home. We can provide for the ever-increasing medical expenses we have with Alexa. This also comes from giving and tithing, which will be discussed more in a future chapter.

> *Dream big, but do it for the Lord!*

After I have gone through my gratitude list, I then think of what I want in the future, and I am grateful for that too. If we are grateful for what we want to be grateful for, we will eventually be grateful for it because it will come. Jesus said, "You may ask me for anything in my name and I will do it" (John 14:14). If my intentions are right with God and in line with His will then my dreams and wishes will be granted. Dream big, but do it for the Lord!

I am grateful for the people in my life who cause me pain and strife. I learn patience from them. I am grateful for the swimming pool in my backyard that isn't there yet because I could use it to fellowship with others and be an example of God to them. The biggest thing I am so grateful for is the cure that is going to be found for Alexa and spinal muscular atrophy.

I feel these things as if they are already done. That is why they will come to me. Everything I have to be grateful for started with a thought or idea. I became emotionally attached to the thought or idea, wanted to use it to please the Lord, and then it became a reality.

★★★★★★★★★★★★★★★★★★★

I wouldn't feel I had served in writing this book if I wrote about gratitude without touching upon grace and blessings. When I am grateful, I start to see God's blessings and grace.

> **When I am grateful, I start to see God's blessings and grace.**

Grace is God's undeserved blessings. I remember when I was a child and something seemingly awful would happen to someone we knew, my parents would always say, "There but for the grace of God go I." I never really understood this until recently. To me it was just a saying. It was like saying, "God bless you," when someone sneezes. It's something many of us say but don't really feel.

"There but for the grace of God go I" means that God has

graced us by not bringing this seemingly bad thing to us. Why did He choose that other person rather than us? Or why did He choose to bless us with something and not someone else? It is His grace.

When we listen to the great American songs and tributes, we hear "God Bless the USA," "God Bless America," and "America the Beautiful" where it says, "God shed his grace on thee." My family and I have truly been blessed to be born and living in America. This became a reality for me when Alexa asked to go to Jerusalem to pray for a cure for her at the tomb of Mary.

We were all so excited to be going on this wonderful spiritual journey. After visiting Jerusalem, we were going to go to Greece for a week "to relax." It was going to be a dream come true for Alexa to go to Jerusalem and my husband to visit the country of his ancestors.

Traveling with Alexa is never as simple as packing a suitcase and getting on a plane. She normally drives a three hundred–pound power wheelchair, but we knew that would not be possible since everything would not be accessible where we were going. We took her manual chair and had to push her everywhere, which took away not only her independence but two of our four adult hands to carry the rest of our things. Alexa also needed to have a bulky, awkward stander with her when she traveled for more than a few days so she could get out of her chair and on her feet. So my husband and I had a standing frame, a suitcase filled with Alexa's medications and supplies, three suitcases of clothes for the next two weeks of travel, a wheelchair to push, and five-year-old Nicole trailing behind with her backpack of airplane activities. What a sight we must have been!

Our first experience was the inaccessibility of airports and the lack of help people were willing to offer. There is no Americans with Disabilities Act (ADA) in Israel or in Greece. So we carried

Alexa and her wheelchair up and down more flights of steps and curbs than I care to ever encounter again. We had to take the wheels off the wheelchair to get it into the tiny cars and the taxis that didn't want to be bothered with us.

As we were on our pilgrimage over the next two weeks, we visited museums, chapels, monasteries, churches, and beaches. Nothing was accessible. We carried Alexa's wheelchair up and down and up and down. It felt like there were five hundred steps going down into the tomb of Mary.

My most memorable experience was dragging her up what seemed to be a million stone steps toward the Acropolis and getting halfway to the top, only to realize it was too steep and narrow to go any farther with the wheelchair. My husband and I stood there for a few minutes, not sure of what to do about the disappointment in Alexa's eyes about not being able to continue. So I picked her up and carried her the rest of the way, knowing she'd probably never get the opportunity to go to the top of the Acropolis again.

We saw many beautiful places on our trip and will probably not ever get to experience Jerusalem again as we did then. Although I thank God for the experiences we had there, we were never so happy to arrive at Kennedy International Airport and set foot on American soil as the day our trip ended.

What I learned most from that experience is how blessed we are to be living in the United States, where we have freedoms not even imagined in other countries. I have an accessible home, a lift van, and the streets have curb cuts. Our children can go to school, get an education, and use computers. My younger daughter, Nicole, went to a non-accessible private school. I used to get angry that Alexa couldn't go there also. Then I remembered being in Greece, where none of the schools are accessible. I think about countries where Alexa would not even be accepted in society, let alone educated. America is a place where women can work and vote. And most importantly, we can worship God. This was all affirmed for a time by the 9/11 disaster that struck our country. Although that was a terrible event and many lives were lost, it helped people realize that God has blessed America, and it is by His grace that we live here. We need to remember our freedoms in the United States and fight to keep them.

If you feel down or hopeless, all you need to do is ask God to grace you, or even show you how He already has, and you will see miracles every day. We all have so much to be grateful for. Just open your eyes and look around you.

What I'd like you to do is start a gratitude list. You may think, *Oh, I have nothing to be grateful for.* Come on, you can think of one thing to be grateful for! Write it down! All day today keep going back to your gratitude list. Anytime a negative thought pops into your head, bring yourself back and say, "I am so grateful for …"

Tomorrow add another thing to your list. And the day after that add another. Keep doing this and you will look back a month from now and find at least thirty things to be grateful for. When my children were young and seemed to be getting ungrateful and taking people and things for granted, I would have them sit down and write a gratitude list.

> **If you're feeling down or hopeless, ask God to show you how He already has blessed you.**

Every time they did this, they came up with more things to be grateful for than the time before. It helped them become more centered and focused on what's really important.

It might be something as simple as, "Thank you for the piece of bread I had for breakfast" to more detail and complexity as I have described in my gratitude list above. Whatever it may be, start writing it here and now! If you need more space, get yourself a journal and keep it with you so when you're going through your day and you think of something to be grateful for, you can write it down.

If you're feeling down or hopeless, ask God to show you how He already has blessed you. If you do this regularly, you will begin to see miracles happen in your life every day. God will find you! I know because it happened to me!

Notes

_____

_____

_____

_____

_____

_____

_____

_____

_____

_____

_____

_____

_____

_____

Chapter 3

Love

When my daughter Alexa was five years old, she was talking on the phone to Wayne Dyer. I heard her ask him, "Why are we here?" I had no idea where this question even came from; it wasn't something she had ever asked me. But then again, she probably already knew that I did not know the answer to this question. The answer that Wayne's wife Marcelene had given was simple, yet so hard to live by. "We are here to know and love God."

Since that time, Marcelene has become such a dear friend and has changed the lives of our whole family with her gentle voice, warmth, and compassion. But mostly what changed our lives was that statement, "We are here to know and love God."

> "We are here to know and love God."

How do we achieve this in a world where children are shooting children with guns? Drugs are on the street corners and in our schools. The schools are having seminars for the kids to teach them about how to recognize abuse and how to stand up for themselves. Oh, and let's not forget the terrorism and bombings occurring all over the world.

I have had to get past my own dysfunctional upbringing and feelings of abandonment and rejection. I remember feeling angry all the time, slamming doors and crying. I did not feel loved, and neither did I love. Sometimes that anger resurfaces, and I need to quickly remind myself of how much God loves me.

I certainly do not consider myself qualified to write this chapter on love. I get angry. I sometimes raise my voice at my children. I have spanked them out of frustration. I am not always patient. I am self-seeking, especially with my time. I am not always kind. I have been known to keep track of my husband's wrongdoings so I can bring them up when I think it will serve my purpose. I brag about my children.

First Corinthians 13 says that love is the opposite of all these things I do. Therefore, I do not feel qualified to be writing about love. So for this chapter I pray even harder than for the others that God speaks through me and shows me His will for these writings.

> Love is patient, love is kind. It does not envy, it does not boast, it is not proud. It does not dishonor others, it is not self-seeking, it is not easily angered, it keeps no record of wrongs. Love does not delight in evil but rejoices with the truth. It always protects, always trusts, always hopes, always perseveres. (1 Corinthian 13:4–7)

If our children feel loved, they will love.

How do we love? How do we teach our children love? If our children feel loved, they will love. If they feel love, they will be more open to God's love for them. They will grow up feeling accepted, not rejected. Therefore, they will accept others as well.

Of course, loving starts with knowing God loves you, but it goes much farther. The Bible says, "But I tell you, love your enemies and pray for those who persecute you" (Matthew 5:44).

Many years ago my husband was trying to help a friend who had gotten hooked on drugs. In the process of this, the drugs had taken over his mind, and he lost all the love he had for anything or anyone, except the drugs. While Peter was trying to help him, in a fit of anger and rage, he got his gun out and was going to shoot Peter.

By the grace of God, Peter got out of the house and called the police from his cell phone. We were quite scared for some time, and the incident made me really think about just how valuable my husband is to me. I almost lost him on that day.

It took Peter and me a long time to get to the point of love with him—to be able to pray for him, to pray that he gets help with his drug problem, for him to open his heart to God and ask forgiveness for his actions, and for him to have peace, faith, love, and gratitude.

> **Love is praying for your enemies.**

Love is praying for your enemies as well as those who mistreat you. I remember when Alexa was in second grade and a little boy was teasing her because she was in a wheelchair. It wasn't just Alexa who had a problem with him. He was nasty to other students and a problem for teachers and administrators. We would pray for God to come into his heart and for this boy to realize that he could be loved. Alexa would cry on the phone to Marcelene about him, and Marcelene would tell her to say to him, "I loved you before you said those things, and I love you now." Eventually, this little boy came around and was no longer a problem in the school. Our praying not only helped by God removing some of the frustrations surrounding this young boy, but it also helped Alexa not feel so hurt and sad because she knew that God was with her and He would help this boy.

I can think of many instances where showing love in the face of adversity is always best, but the most significant in my mind is with my in-laws. For the first several years of our marriage, the conflict with them was relentless. I felt like no matter what I did, they wouldn't like me. We were constantly bucking heads and arguing over something. I had not yet accepted Christ into my life and had a very large ego. It only got worse when my children were born, because they were, after all, "my children." I remember having such an argument with them and I wouldn't let them see my children for months. I had so much anger and hatred in my heart for them. It was eating away at me and was destructive to everyone involved.

After I allowed the Lord into my heart and began to practice this principle of love, I began to find peace. I started to ask myself, "How would God want me to treat my in-laws?" If our purpose of being here on earth is to know and love God, then I need to fully and completely love others. We cannot love God fully and have anger for others. If we show people we love them when they feel they don't deserve it, they will find love.

As a result of this change in my heart and in my thinking, I truly do love my in-laws. One summer my father in-law and I had said some unkind words to one another. I was able to call him and say to him, "I don't want to hurt you. God put you in my life because He wants me to love you, and I do love you very much. I don't want to fight with you. I'm sorry."

The Bible says, "Do everything in love" (1 Corinthians 16:14). This also refers to unconditional love. Kaye O'Bara showed this love with her daughter, Edwarda. Edwarda had been in a coma for over thirty years. Kaye cared for her in their home until her passing. Edwarda had never had a bedsore and was fed through a feeding tube every two hours around the clock due to diabetes. Kaye had dedicated her life to caring for Edwarda. This is unconditional love. It is the love most mothers have for their children.

Now go beyond your children and think about if you could love an outsider as much as you love your own children. Would you stop to help a person on the street who has a maimed face? Would you give a stranger food or money? Would you do as Mother Theresa did every day and go into the streets of Calcutta and do a deed for someone you never met just to let them know they are loved?

Jesus said, "Love one another. As I have loved you, so you must love one another" (John 13:34). If Jesus loved me more than His own soul and His own life, then I need to strive to love others that much. Jesus didn't care that others persecuted Him. He just prayed for them.

I am going to close this chapter on love with this:

> Love must be sincere. Hate what is evil; cling to what is good. Be devoted to one another in love. Honor one another above yourselves. Never be lacking in zeal, but keep your spiritual fervor, serving the Lord. Be joyful in hope, patient in affliction, faithful in prayer. Share with the Lord's people who are in need. Practice hospitality. Bless those who persecute you; bless and do not curse. Rejoice with those who rejoice; mourn with those who mourn. Live in harmony with one another. Do not be proud, but be willing to associate with people of low position. Do not be conceited. Do not repay anyone evil for evil. Be careful to do what is right in the eyes of everyone. If it is possible, as far as it depends on you, live at peace with everyone. Do not take revenge, my dear friends, but leave room for God's wrath, for it is written: "It is mine to avenge; I will repay," says the Lord. On the contrary: "If your enemy is hungry, feed him; if he is thirsty, give him something to drink. In doing this, you will heap burning coals on his head." Do not be overcome by evil, but overcome evil with good. (Romans 12:9–21)

Notes

Chapter 4

Service

How can I serve? I try to ask this question many times throughout the day, from the time my alarm clock goes off in the morning and I just want one more minute to sleep, until the time I go to bed and ask, "Have I served today?"

Service cannot be done from my laziness in my bed just buying one more, and one more, and one more minute before my feet hit the floor. When my alarm goes off, my feet need to hit the floor in order for service to begin.

> **Ask yourself every day, "How can I serve?"**

My typical day starts on my elliptical or bike, where I am serving. I am serving because I listen to praise music or watch sermons and church services on TV. These bring me closer to God. I am also serving because I am treating my body as a temple and caring for it in the way God would want me to. I am serving because at this time I go through my gratitude list and remember everything I am grateful for and the things I want to be grateful for.

My service then moves on to how I treat my family. How do I talk to them? How do I treat them all day long? If I have pleased God, then I have done my job for that day and I have served.

Sometimes kids don't want to get up in the morning. Sometimes they talk back. They even argue among each other. How do I handle these situations every day? I ask the question, "How can I serve?" and the answer comes. It doesn't always come immediately, and sometimes I have to walk away from them, but if I'm even half as patient with God as He's been with me, He will send me answers.

I have posted on a piece of paper in my daily reading, "In all that I do, serve the Lord." If what I am doing is pleasing to God, then I am serving.

> **In all that I do, serve the Lord.**

We all have spiritual gifts given to us by God. Some gifts may be teaching, encouraging, leading, writing, creativity, or athleticism. No matter what our gifts are, it is our responsibility to use them to serve others and glorify God. The Bible says:

> We have different gifts, according to the grace given to each of us. If your gift is prophesying, then prophesy in accordance with your faith; if it is serving, then serve; if it is teaching, then teach; if it is to encourage, then give encouragement; if it is giving, then give generously; if it is to lead, do it diligently; if it is to show mercy, do it cheerfully. (Romans 12:6–8)

All of these things are ways of service to others.

Serving is following your dreams if your dreams are in alignment with God's will. I have the strong belief that you don't mess with other people's dreams. I just pray that they align their dreams with what God wants. We taught Alexa to never let her disability get in the way of her dreams. Dream big! As a result of this, Alexa has graduated from college and at the time of this writing, is considering law school in California. We live in Pennsylvania, mind you. Needless to say, we are all very scared about this. We went to California and everything was falling into place at the law school Alexa was looking at. Scholarship, accommodations, and housing are all major factors to consider, especially when you're in a wheelchair. After we had looked at the school, Alexa said that maybe it wasn't the school for her. I didn't quite understand this since the school

Serving is following your dreams if your dreams are in alignment with God's will.

had agreed to all our major conditions. After I thought about it, the word *fear* popped into my mind.

I said something like this to Alexa: "I think you are having doubts about this school because you are afraid. You have dreamed of living in California since you were thirteen years old. For the last two years this has been your first-choice law school. We did not raise you to not do something because you are afraid. I would like you to look at your dreams and really listen to God and to your heart. If you feel God is telling you not to go here because it is His will, that is one thing. But if it is out of fear, that is another."

When I think of the reasons for Alexa having SMA I am reminded of Jesus and the blind man. "'Neither this man nor his parents sinned,' said Jesus, 'but this happened so that the work of God might be displayed in his life'" (John 9:3).

I hate the thought of either of my children being on the other side of the country, but if that is where the Lord

Let go and let God! He has a plan!

needs them, then I need to let go and let God! He has a plan!

Something to be very mindful of while you are serving is your reason behind your service. The ego is a very powerful act of Satan. *Ego* stands for edging God out. We cannot serve God and our ego at the same time. I have caught myself thinking I am serving for the Lord when I am really serving to boost my own ego or feeling of accomplishment. For years I have been

We cannot serve God and our ego at the same time.

delivering Meals on Wheels to elderly people who cannot get to the grocery store or prepare their own meals. There are many days I return from my deliveries and have gotten so much from the gratitude of these elderly people. I have to remind myself that it is not about what they are giving me, but what God would want me to give them.

My husband and his family have been great teachers in the area of service and financial giving. They were always very generous and gave anonymously. Again, my ego comes into play and I have to look to where Jesus said, "Be careful not to practice your righteousness in front of others to be seen by them. If you do, you will have no reward from your Father in heaven" (Matthew 6:1). And, "But when you give to the needy, do not let your left hand know what your right hand is doing, so that your giving may be in secret. Then your Father, who sees what is done in secret, will reward you" (Matthew 6:3–4).

I often think of these verses when I think of my in-laws and how they gave unconditionally and anonymously. My husband and I have been tithing for many years, and we teach our children to tithe also. Tithing is giving 10 percent of all our income to God. We believe in doing this for two reasons. First, it is because the Bible says give a tenth of all God has given you back to Him. Second, our church community is so vital to who we are that we need to support and nurture it financially so it can continue to give back to others and us. When I tithe and give offerings, I need to keep my ego in check and remember that I am giving not for recognition or even the reward from God. I am giving out of love for God. I love Him so much that I want to please Him. I know He is pleased when I serve others with my time, talent, and money.

I remember when I was working on my MBA we had an entire class discussion on serving and the statement, "Don't ever ask someone to do something that you yourself are not willing to do." I don't ask someone to clean my toilets if I am not willing to do it. I would not ask someone to clean the dog's poop if I was not willing to do it. This is part of serving. Jesus would never ask something of us that He would not do. He even washed His disciples' feet, telling them to wash one another's feet. Now that is serving!

The Bible says, "For it is by grace you have been saved, through faith—and this is not from yourselves, it is the gift of God—not by works, so that no one can boast" (Ephesians 2:8–9).

I know from this verse that no matter how much I serve, it is not what will give me eternal life. It is God's grace that gives me eternal life.

Serve joyfully. Now it is one thing to serve. It is another to serve joyfully. The Lord has blessed us with a wonderful house that we can share with others. The summer we started building the house was the same summer I became a believer in Christ. That was no coincidence. I truly believe it is not my house. It is God's house, and He is letting us use it for a time for His glory.

Serve joyfully.

Because our home is wheelchair accessible for Alexa, it just always made sense for me to have the holidays and events. We have the go-to house for the family holidays, celebrations, and many youth events with sometimes more than seventy-five people in attendance. I do most of the preparing, setting up, and cooking for these events. Thankfully, many attendees often share the clean up! Oftentimes, especially near the holidays when I am exhausted from preparations, I need to remind myself to serve joyfully. I also remember, "I can do all through him who gives me strength" (Philippians 4:13).

Jesus says, "Give and it will be given to you" (Luke 6:38). I truly believe this. My husband and I often say, "We keep what we have by giving it away." Tithing is serving. Serving is tithing. There were many times when we didn't know how we were going to pay the bills, but God always came through. And we need to come through for Him by giving of our time, talents, and money.

We keep what we have by giving it away.

I heard maybe some twenty years ago, although I don't remember where, "Live your life so your life outlives you." Hence, the reason God has led me to write this book. It started out to be something to leave behind for my children. God will make it more than that if He chooses. If you are living for yourself and not for God and others, you will not be remembered. Live your life to make a difference to the world. If I die knowing I have served God in all that I have done, then I have lived!

If I die knowing I have served God in all that I have done, then I have lived!

Notes

_____

_____

_____

_____

_____

_____

_____

_____

_____

_____

_____

_____

Notes

Chapter 5

Prayer and Meditation

When we write about or teach something, our expertise comes from our experiences. Yes, I read my Bible, and yes, I pray. But I hardly feel that I am a prayer worrier or that I read and pray nearly enough.

I often look to others for guidance in this area, especially since I wasn't raised in a praying family. Since the day I met my husband, he has had the routine of kneeling in prayer every morning. We have a chapel off of our bedroom, and he goes in there alone and kneels before God. Sometimes he's in there so long I think he fell asleep praying, but when I peek in, I can see how wrong I am. On the rare days that I am awake at his ridiculous hour of 4:00 a.m., I will join him in the chapel and he will pray aloud. When I listen to him pray, I become grateful for him. I am certain that our children are as healthy and happy as they are because of his diligent praying!

When I think of Peter in the chapel praying every morning, it reminds me of what Jesus said.

> And when you pray, do not be like the hypocrites, for they love to pray standing in the synagogues and on the street corners to be seen by others. Truly I tell you, they have received their reward in full. But when you pray, go into your room, close the door and pray to your Father, who is unseen. (Matthew 6:5–6)

Although I enjoy my time in our chapel on my knees praying to Jesus, my praying doesn't start or end there. We have visited many monasteries and spoken with many monks and nuns over the years. They are by far the most peaceful and loving people I have ever encountered in my life. They have taught me to endeavor to pray without ceasing, as Paul wrote, "pray continually" (1 Thessalonians 5:17). They are striving to pray continuously while they are not only in church services but while they do their work all day long. They continuously pray the Jesus Prayer, "Lord, Jesus Christ, Son of God, have mercy on me, a sinner."[1]

We all have sin in us since the day Eve ate that apple off the tree. We are not perfect. The only one who was ever perfect is Jesus. In order to know and love God (remember, that's why we are here), we need to strive to be like Jesus even though we know we never can be. The way to do this is through prayer. Praising God, confessing our sins to God, giving thanks to God, and asking for His mercy. God listens!

In order to know and love God, we need to strive to be like Jesus even though we know we never can be.

It is truly amazing how prayer opens our eyes to the miracles before us every day. I have seen many miracles after praying. Seeing Mary appear before me in Jerusalem is one for sure!

Whenever we get into our car for a long drive, we begin by making the sign of the cross. On one particular occasion, the kids and I were in North Carolina visiting with my brother and his family. We decided to leave to come home at 6:00 p.m. to avoid traffic. We got in the car, crossed ourselves, and started driving. After a couple of Starbucks to keep us awake, we needed to make a pit stop. It was around midnight, and we were in the middle of nowhere. In our family, we call it Jabip. We pulled off into a rest area.

It is truly amazing how prayer opens our eyes to the miracles before us every day.

There were only two cars in the parking lot. Now, I was a little scared, but we all really had to pee! Nicole and I got out of the car and unloaded Alexa in her wheelchair, and man was it dark. As we started walking toward the bathroom, two men got out of their car and started walking also. Keep in mind, the car was already sitting there when we pulled in. They were waiting for us. We got about one hundred feet from the car, and they started saying, "Hey, girls, how are you doin'?" Nicole, Alexa, and I stopped dead in our tracks and looked at each other. Remember, we really had to go! And now we were petrified that these creepy guys were going to rape and/or kill us. At that very moment a policeman pulled into the parking lot. I walked up to him and asked him to stick around for a few minutes while we used the facilities because we were afraid of those guys. He said no problem. That was a miracle. There is no doubt in my mind that God sent that policeman at that very moment to watch over us and protect us. He put us there and showed us a miracle!

Not only does prayer open us to see miracles in our lives, but it also opens our hearts and minds to seeing God's will for us. God gave a miracle and showed His will for us during Alexa's sophomore year in college. She was in a Washington, DC, Children's Hospital ICU with a respiratory infection. We seriously thought she was going to die. We pulled Nicole, then a high school senior, out of school so she could be

Prayer opens our heart and mind to seeing God's will for us.

with us in DC. On the worst night of Alexa's illness when I was sure we were going to lose her, I started praying. While I was praying, I remembered Abraham's love for God in Genesis 22. He loved God so much he was willing to sacrifice his son, Isaac. I prayed that if it was God's will to take Alexa then so be it—that I trusted His decision and loved Him enough to give her up to Him. Again I would see a miracle in my most exhausted state. We called the doctor into the room. She sat with us for two hours and worked on Alexa, clearing mucous to keep her alive. God sent us another miracle. Most doctors would call in a respiratory therapist to do that job. Not this time. She did it herself until Alexa was out of trouble.

From what seemed to be one of the worst moments in my life came some of life's lessons. Nicole decided she wanted to serve God by becoming a nurse. I realized just how much I love God and was reminded how much He loves me.

Just to keep things in perspective, less than one month after this event, Peter got sick and was in the hospital. I was not willing to pray the same prayer regarding my husband. God put me in my place after my feeling of righteous indignation.

When we pray, we need to believe with all our hearts that God hears us and knows what is best for us. In the Bible the father of a demon-possessed boy says to Jesus, "I do believe; help me overcome my unbelief!" (Mark 9:24). I love this verse because it shows that even though we may be a believer in what the Lord it capable of, we are not perfect believers. The devil and doubt creep in like thieves in the night. We need to pray daily for God to strengthen our belief in Him and overcome our doubts and unbelief to achieve complete faith.

Because prayer helps us see the miracles God performs in our lives, never stop praying for more miracles. Alexa was diagnosed with SMA at sixteen months. I still pray for a cure. Just because there isn't a cure yet doesn't mean God can't cure her. It means it's just not time. He can do anything. Jesus says, "With God all things are possible" (Matthew 19:26). I truly believe He has not cured her because she still has something to learn or something to teach while she is in a wheelchair.

Prayer also helps us to forgive others. Holding on to anger and animosity does not hurt the person we are angry with. It only hurts ourselves.

Notes

Notes

Chapter 6

Overall Wellness and Balance

As previously stated, our ultimate goal in life is to know and love God. We can only achieve this if our physical, spiritual, and mental selves are balanced. When we are balanced, we are at peace because we will know and love God more fully. The previous four chapters addressed the mental and spiritual aspects of balance. We will now address the physical portion of this balance, which includes exercise and nutrition.

Exercise reduces stress, helps with focus, and aids in weight loss.

As I have mentioned before, I start most of my days on my elliptical or my bike. I have ADD and auditory processing problems. Concentrating is extremely difficult for me. I need to exercise to change the chemical makeup in my brain in order to help me concentrate and reduce my stress level.

In addressing the issue of stress, Dr. Peter J. D'Adamo in his book *Eat Right for your Type* describes the results of stress as follows:

> Stress-related disorders cause 50 to 80 percent of all illnesses in modern life. We know how powerfully the mind influences the body and the body influences the mind. The entire range of these interactions is still being explored.

Problems known to be exacerbated by stress and the mind-body connection are ulcers, high blood pressure, heart disease, migraine headaches, arthritis and other inflammatory diseases, asthma and other respiratory diseases, insomnia and other sleep disorders, and a variety of skin problems ranging from hives to herpes, from eczema to psoriasis. Stress is disastrous to the immune system, leaving the body open to a myriad of opportunistic health problems. ... The body's response to stress has been developed and refined over thousands of years. It is a reflex, an animal instinct, our survival mechanism for dealing with life-or-death situations. When danger of any kind is sensed, we mobilize our fight-or-flight response, and we either confront what is alarming us or flee from it—mentally or physically.[2]

I love to watch weight loss shows such as *The Biggest Loser* and Chris Powell's *Extreme Weight Loss*, especially while I am working out. The underlying theme of almost every episode of these shows is that the result of being overweight can lead to the following problems:

- high blood pressure
- diabetes
- heart attacks
- strokes
- sleep disorders

These shows teach us to honor our bodies. We need to honor our bodies so we can honor Christ.

Paul says:

> Do you not know that your body is a temple of
> the Holy Spirit, who is in you, whom you have
> received from God? You are not your own; you
> were brought at a price. Therefore honor God
> with your bodies. (1 Corinthians 6:19–20)

> Don't you know that you yourselves are God's
> temple and that God's Spirit dwells in your
> midst? If anyone destroys God's temple, God
> will destroy that person; for God's temple is
> sacred, and you together are that temple. (1
> Corinthians 3:16–17)

I always keep the above verses in mind because my ADD is
not only affected by exercise but also by what I eat. When I eat
heavy carbs and gluten, my brain is fuzzy.
The most common temptation many face
is eating food that makes them feel bad.
By defeating this temptation, we will feel
physically and emotionally better. The
Christlike qualities we can more fully
develop are love, patience, and kindness. Eating right helps put
the physical piece of our wheel into balance.

We need to honor our bodies so we can honor Christ.

Another important thing to remember is that, according to
HH Mitchel in the *Journal of Biological Chemistry* (158), our brains
and hearts are composed of 73 percent water.[3] God created us
this way, and we honor Him every time we drink a glass of
water. We also need to give thanks for our clean water since it is
a blessing not given to every country.

The Bible says:

> All these I have kept," the young man said. "What do I still lack?" Jesus answered, "If you want to be perfect, go, sell your possessions and give to the poor, and you will have treasure in heaven. Then come, follow me." (Matthew 19:20–21)

The man Jesus was speaking to had the love of possessions. Give up what consumes you, whether it be possessions, alcohol, drugs, sex, pornography, or food. What is addiction? It is never getting enough of what we don't want or shouldn't have. What is the thing you crave or want more than Jesus? I take a good look at this every year during the Lenten season. Following is my Lenten action plan, which gets posted on my bathroom mirror the week before Lent starts every year.

> *Give up what consumes you. What is the thing you crave or want more than Jesus?*

****

My Lenten Action Plan
Forty Days for Christ

1. Fasting from wheat, sugar, social media, and phone games
2. Under 1,500 calories per day
3. Work out minimum of four times per week
4. Pray in chapel minimum of five times per week

By eliminating these things of the world and focusing on Christ, I will become closer to Him!

★★★★★★★★★★

When I am following this plan, my mind is far more open to Jesus.

The things listed under number 1 are the things that consume me and pull me away from Christ the most. This is a plan that should be followed all year long. I have not yet come to the point of willingness in that arena. Also, the first year I made this list, Starbucks was on it under number 1. Well ... once was enough for that. I'm definitely a work in progress. Practice makes progress! I started with this plan many years ago during Lent. I now follow it for the forty days before Christmas also.

> *Practice makes progress!*

In our house the definition of insanity is repeating the same thing and expecting different results. There is a story about a person who kept going down the same road and falling in a hole. Choose a different road—a different path. That is why I chose this Lenten Action Plan.

God wants to use me as a messenger. It is my job to put myself in a place where I can receive that message so I can read, write, pray, and serve. If I would have continued on my same path and not chosen the path of Christ I would never have achieved the peace and balance I have today.

My best writing comes when I am praying and fasting. I pray (and listen) better when I am fasting. And I fast better when I am praying. I cannot effectively do either unless I exercise.

Our ultimate goal is to know and love God. We cannot do this if we are stressed and not honoring our bodies. If we are stressed, we cannot maintain balance. If we cannot maintain balance, we will be stressed. We need to not only balance our physical selves but mental and spiritual also.

How do you react to stress? Following is a summary of the points to reducing stress and achieving physical, mental, and spiritual balance:

- Maintain a close relationship with God by praying regularly and reading the Bible daily.
- Love deeply and sincerely.
- Recognize our blessings, and give thanks for them.
- Exercise four to five times a week.
- Eat healthy foods in healthy quantities.
- Maintain a healthy weight.
- Serve God in all you do.

And remember, practice makes progress. We are not perfect. We cannot be perfect. The only perfect one is Jesus. Just keep practicing and progressing to maintain physical, mental, and spiritual balance.

When we can't find God, God finds us. He is seeking you out even when you can't seek Him!

I was lost, but God found me. When we can't find God, God finds us, just as He has many times in my life, as I have written about in this book. Keep your heart and mind open and ready. God is with you, and He is seeking you out even when you can't seek Him!

Notes

Notes

Bible Verses by Chapter

Chapter 2: Gratitude—Giving Thanks

John 14:14: "You may ask me for anything in my name and I will do it."

Chapter 3: Love

1 Corinthians 13:4–7: Love is patient, love is kind. It does not envy, it does not boast, it is not proud. It does not dishonor others, it is not self-seeking, it is not easily angered, it keeps no record of wrongs. Love does not delight in evil but rejoices with the truth. It always protects, always trusts, always hopes, always perseveres.

Matthew 5:44: "But I tell you, love your enemies and pray for those who persecute you."

1 Corinthians 16:14: Do everything in love.

John 13:34: "Love one another. As I have loved you, so you must love one another."

Romans 12:9–21: Love must be sincere. Hate what is evil; cling to what is good. Be devoted to one another in love. Honor one another above yourselves. Never be lacking in zeal, but keep your spiritual fervor, serving the Lord. Be joyful in hope, patient in affliction, faithful in prayer. Share with the Lord's people who are in need. Practice hospitality

Bless those who persecute you; bless and do not curse. Rejoice with those who rejoice; mourn with those who mourn. Live in harmony with one another. Do not be proud, but be willing to associate with people of low position. Do not be conceited.

Do not repay anyone evil for evil. Be careful to do what is right in the eyes of everyone. If it is possible, as far as it depends on you, live at peace with everyone. Do not take revenge, my dear friends, but leave room for God's wrath, for it is written: "It is mine to avenge; I will repay," says the Lord. On the contrary: "If your enemy is hungry, feed him; if he is thirsty, give him something to drink. In doing this, you will heap burning coals on his head." Do not be overcome by evil, but overcome evil with good.

Chapter 4: Service

Romans 12:6–8: We have different gifts, according to the grace given to each of us. If your gift is prophesying, then prophesy in accordance with your faith; if it is serving, then serve; if it is teaching, then teach; if it is to encourage, then give encouragement; if it is giving, then give generously; if it is to show mercy, do it cheerfully.

John 9:3: "Neither this man nor his parents sinned," said Jesus, "but this happened so that the work of God might be displayed in his life."

Matthew 6:1: "Be careful not to practice your righteousness in front of others to be seen by them. If you do, you will have no reward from your Father in heaven."

Matthew 6:3–4: "But when you give to the needy, do not let your left hand know what your right hand is doing, so that your giving may be in secret. Then your Father, who sees what is done in secret, will reward you."

Ephesians 2:8–9: For it is by grace you have been saved, through faith—and this is not from yourselves, it is the gift of God— not by works, so that no one can boast.

Philippians 4:13: I can do all through him who gives me strength.

Luke 6:38: "Give and it will be given to you ..."

Chapter 5: Prayer and Meditation

Matthew 6:5–6: "And when you pray, do not be like the hypocrites, for they love to pray standing in the synagogues and on the street corners to be seen by others. Truly I tell you, they have received their reward in full. But when you pray, go into your room, close the door and pray to your Father, who is unseen ..."

1 Thessalonians 5:17: Pray continually.

Mark 9:24: "I do believe; help me overcome my unbelief!"

Matthew 19:26: "With God all things are possible."

Chapter 6: Overall Wellness and Balance

1 Corinthians 6:19–20: Do you not know that your body is a temple of the Holy Spirit, who is in you, whom you have received from God? You are not your own; you were brought at a price. Therefore honor God with your bodies.

1 Corinthians 3:16–17: Don't you know that you yourselves are God's temple and that God's Spirit dwells in your midst? If anyone destroys God's temple, God will destroy that person; for God's temple is sacred, and you together are that temple.

Matthew 19:20–21: "All these I have kept," the young man said. "What do I still lack?" Jesus answered, "If you want to be perfect, go, sell your possessions and give to the poor, and you will have treasure in heaven. Then come, follow me."

Things to Remember by Chapter

Chapter 2: Gratitude—Giving Thanks

1. Sometimes what we think might be a bad thing is really just God's wake-up call to have us take a look at our life and how we are living it.
2. Dream big, but do it for the Lord!
3. When I am grateful, I start to see God's blessings and grace.
4. If you're feeling down or hopeless, ask God to show you how He already has blessed you.

Chapter 3: Love

1. "We are here to know and love God."
2. If our children feel loved, they will love.
3. Love is praying for your enemies.

Chapter 4: Service

1. Ask yourself every day, "How can I serve?"
2. In all that I do, serve the Lord.
3. Serving is following your dreams if your dreams are in alignment with God's will.
4. Let go and let God! He has a plan!
5. We cannot serve God and our ego at the same time.

6. Serve joyfully.
7. We keep what we have by giving it away.
8. If I die knowing I have served God in all that I have done, then I have lived!

Chapter 5: Prayer and Meditation

1. In order to know and love God, we need to strive to be like Jesus even though we know we never can be.
2. It is truly amazing how prayer opens our eyes to the miracles before us every day.
3. Prayer opens our hearts and minds to seeing God's will for us.

Chapter 6: Overall Wellness and Balance

1. We need to honor our bodies so we can honor Christ.
2. Give up what consumes you. What is the thing you crave or want more than Jesus?
3. Practice makes progress!
4. When we can't find God, God finds us. He is seeking you out even when you can't seek Him!

Notes

1. Greek Orthodox Archdiocese of America, "The Jesus Prayer," Web. August 11, 2015. http://www.goarch.org/ourfaith/ourfaith7104
2. Dr. Peter J. D'Adamo, *Eat Right for Your Type*. (New York: G.P. Putnam's Sons, 1996), 41–43.
3. H. H. Mitchell, T.S Hamilton, F.R. Steggerda, and H.W. Bean. "The Chemical Composition of the Adult Human Body and the Biochemistry of Growth." *The Journal of Biological Chemistry* 158 (1945): 625–37.

Dear Readers,

Thank you so much for reading my book. I would love hear how God has found you. Please visit my website, www.juliedectis.com

May God find you wherever you are!
Julie Dectis

About Julie Dectis

Some people say, "God laughs when we make plans." That is certainly what He was doing while Julie Dectis was finishing her engineering degree. She had her life planned out. She would soon be rising to the top in her career, getting married, starting a family, and living out the perfect American life. Shortly after marrying her husband and having her first child, Julie's plans were turned upside down when her baby was diagnosed with spinal muscular atrophy, a rare neuromuscular disease. Angry, depressed, and overwhelmed, Julie had no idea that God had a much bigger plan to bring her close to Him. Through pain and heartbreak, Julie gave her life to God and was able to flourish. Today, she spends her time speaking and writing about her experiences, while giving all glory to God for bringing her to the light.

Julie has been married to Peter for over twenty-five years. They work side by side within their painting business in Pennsylvania. Together they have two daughters, Alexa and Nicole.

Printed in the United States
By Bookmasters